# Raptor World
# Owls

by Jenna Lee Gleisner

Bullfrog Books

# Ideas for Parents and Teachers

Bullfrog Books let children practice reading informational text at the earliest reading levels. Repetition, familiar words, and photo labels support early readers.

## Before Reading

- Discuss the cover photo. What does it tell them?

- Look at the picture glossary together. Read and discuss the words.

## Read the Book

- "Walk" through the book and look at the photos. Let the child ask questions. Point out the photo labels.

- Read the book to the child, or have him or her read independently.

## After Reading

- Prompt the child to think more. Ask: Owls have good eyesight to hunt at night. Can you think of other animals that have special abilities that help them hunt?

Bullfrog Books are published by Jump!
5357 Penn Avenue South
Minneapolis, MN 55419
www.jumplibrary.com

Library of Congress Cataloging-in-Publication Data

Names: Gleisner, Jenna Lee, author.
Title: Owls / by Jenna Lee Gleisner.
Description: Bullfrog books edition.
Minneapolis, MN : Jump!, Inc., [2020]
Series; Raptor World
Audience: Age 5-8. | Audience: K to Grade 3.
Includes index.
Identifiers: LCCN 2018038132 (print)
LCCN 2018039067 (ebook)
ISBN 9781641286350 (e-book)
ISBN 9781641286343 (hardcover : alk. paper)
ISBN 9781641288248 (pbk.)
Subjects: LCSH: Owls—Juvenile literature.
Classification: LCC QL696.S83 (ebook)
LCC QL696.S83 G58 2020 (print)
DDC 598.9/7—dc23
LC record available at https://lccn.loc.gov/2018038132

Editor: Susanne Bushman
Designer: Jenna Casura

Photo Credits: anankkml/iStock, cover; GlobalP/iStock, 1; pchoui/iStock, 3; NFKenyon/Shutterstock, 4, 23tl; Jasper Doest/Minden Pictures/SuperStock, 5; Gary C. Tognoni/Shutterstock, 6–7; Alan Tunnicliffe/Shutterstock, 8–9; Nick Vorobey/Shutterstock, 10–11, 23br; J & C Sohns/Tier und Naturfotografie/SuperStock, 12–13; FJAH/Shutterstock, 14 (foreground), 23bl; Marina Barysheva/Shutterstock, 14 (background), 23bl; Eric Isselee/Shutterstock, 15, 22; fotolincs/Alamy, 16–17, 23tr; Horst Jegen/imageBROKER/SuperStock, 18; Ondrej Prosicky/Shutterstock, 19; John Gooday/Minden Pictures/SuperStock, 20–21; artisteer/iStock, 24.

Printed in the United States of America at Corporate Graphics in North Mankato, Minnesota.

# Table of Contents

# Quiet Hunters

It is dark.

An owl peers
through the forest.

It sits.

It waits.

Owls can see well.
Even at night.
This is when they hunt.
Cool!

What was that noise?
An owl turns its head.
It turns almost all
the way around!

Owls hear well, too.
It hears a vole.

vole

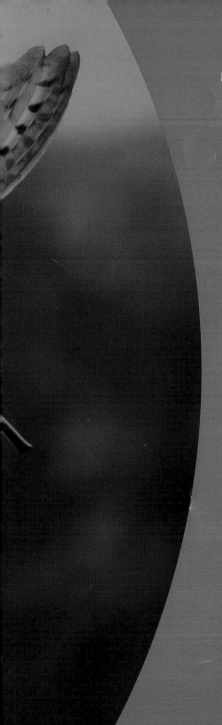

The owl takes off.

It is quiet.

The vole can't hear it.

It stretches out its talons.

They are sharp!

talon

Swoop!
The owl grabs its prey.
It carries it away.

Its beak is also sharp.
It helps the owl eat.
Owls eat insects.

beak

Fish, too.

# What does this owl see?

# Built to Hunt

**wings**
Large wings help owls float through the air without having to flap much. They are such quiet fliers that they can still hear prey while flying.

**beak**
The beak is hooked and sharp. This helps the owl tear and eat prey.

**talons**
Sharp talons help owls grab, carry, and hold onto prey. They also wrap around branches to help owls perch in trees.

**feathers**
Special feathers absorb sound so owls can fly right next to their prey without being heard. An owl's feather color and design camouflage the owl, helping it hide and hunt.

# Picture Glossary

**peers**
Looks curiously.

**prey**
Animals that are hunted
by other animals for food.

**swoop**
To rush down upon
something suddenly.

**vole**
A small, mouselike rodent.

# Index

# To Learn More

**Finding more information is as easy as 1, 2, 3.**

❶ Go to www.factsurfer.com

❷ Enter "owls" into the search box.

❸ Click the "Surf" button to see a list of websites.

24